To a Nurse Friend Weeping

Poems by

Francis Christian

HARP Publishing
The People's Press
Clydesdale, Nova Scotia
Canada

HARP: The People's Press
216 Clydesdale Road
Clydesdale, Nova Scotia
Canada B2G 2K9

www.harppublishing.ca

Information about purchasing copies of this book can be obtained from the publishers

harppeoplespress@gmail.com

tel. 902-863-0396

Catalogue-in-Publication data is on file with the Library and Archives Canada

ISBN: 978-1-990137-05-1

Cover photographs by Author
Graphic design: Cathy Lin
Author portrait: Jebarani Christian

To J.C.
- who knows how much I love her

Dr. Francis Christian is a surgeon, a poet, and a humanist. He has successfully incorporated the humanities as a synergistic element into his academic surgical practice and his life. He has been a role model for a new generation of surgeons as the Director of the Surgical Humanities Program at the University of Saskatchewan. The incorporation of the humanities expressed by visual arts, music, and poetry into the practice of surgeons has enriched our activities both within and outside the operating room and has made us better surgeons.

With this book of poems, Francis Christian reveals an inner sensibility that is rarely expressed by members of our trade. It is precisely that humanistic sensibility that needs to be an integral part of the practice of surgery. Medicine is a profession of service to others — our patients. Incorporating a humanistic approach to this service is essential to us as surgeons and as human beings.

Ivar Mendez, MD, PhD, FRCSC, FACS, FCAHS
F.H. Wigmore Professor and Provincial Head of Surgery
University of Saskatchewan and Saskatchewan Health Authority

Francis Christian has put together a wonderful collection of poems. It is not just that they embody the rarest thing in poetry: an original voice. It is their vigour and variety that so impresses: his very sensitive love poems side by side with poems that tremble with an awareness of human suffering, as well as deeply religious poems that come as a refreshing surprise in the brutally realistic landscape that we all inhabit in these "no nonsense" times.

Francis Christian has a real lyrical gift, but it is lyricism with an iron core. His poems do not plead for our attention but speak full out with the authority of a dedicated artist.

We are fortunate indeed to have such a poet in our midst.

Henry Woolf, Shakespearian actor

Francis Christian in his book of poems gives us the mind of a man who has created a welcome fusion between the disciplines of the sciences and the humanities through a Christian vision of the world. These poems speak of an evolving world, wherein our human nature continues to struggle with the irony of good and evil, and to live the story of the Fall and Redemption. Within this framework the poems describe in vivid detail the ecstasy of making love and the tragedy of the ravages of war. There is also space within the broad reach of the book to celebrate the landscapes of Canada, and the bravery of a little bird that winters over in the frozen north, to scorn the Mustang and deny the I-phone, to praise the beauty in our world and in our lives. In short, the book represents the thinking of a poet who brings to life the theology of the Incarnation.

Professor Robert Sider - Dickinson University and University of Saskatchewan. Classical scholar, author, translator into English of the complete works of Erasmus

Preface

The encounter with suffering cannot be said to be different in substance for physicians from that which is experienced by other human beings in a world where the spectre of suffering seems never far from us.

Nor must it be assumed that because I am a surgeon, the poems and songs I have composed are especially close to the human condition. I am all too aware that every individual's experience of that which we call life is imbued and endowed with its own special, unique stamp and story.

Physicians simply approach illness of mind, body and soul in a manner informed by prior experience, knowledge and training — and importantly, with every grinding reminder of mortality, we share with everyone else, a yearning for a better world and a new order of things.

The reader will therefore discern quickly and quite clearly in many of these poems, I hope, both the all too present story of suffering and hope for a better tomorrow.

Such consequential and searing experiences as love and beauty in our universe, must have the thread of eternity running through them. A certain deep sensibility, like notes however faintly heard from an Angel's harp, assures us that this is so. I hope my poems will awaken for the reader this precious sensibility, never far from us and always reminding us of that which we cannot yet clearly see.

TO A NURSE FRIEND WEEPING*

Forever it may seem you feel
the fevered brow
burning on cool fingers;
and wish you could not wonder
at wonder being put to sleep
beneath midnight stars
that shine so severally deep
and cold in the misty skies.
Twinkle of knowledge
of not knowing what you know
or feeling of feeling
what you feel —
of being left random alone
in the gentle night
heavy with air of
tonight snuffed out
from light of tomorrow
and the meaning of
meaning turned on its head.

* at the side of her just dead, young patient

It may seem this sorrow
has seamless resources
to sap the soft touch
of your soul upon
the next fevered brow
or trembling hand.
And the mask of now
may hide the face of tomorrow
from even your gentle eyes.

I don't believe belief
can breathe its broad
store of reasons
of why you must still believe
down your moist neck;
why even its entry
into this grim hall…
may make you rise and leave.
Not that you have not wrested
from rising vapours of
various "whys" your own
versions of purpose.

Or struggled to seek
in the steaming mists
of burning tears
(yours and hers and theirs)
the source of their flow —
as the pilgrim still seeks
the Ganges at its source.

That the Maker must
make do with cosmic dust;
and bear blood and
bruised body beaten blue
to the shivering hill
and shout out clear
whilst cosmic metal
holds him fast
that it "is finished."
What done? What at an end?
— This order of things
the way things are
the way they must not be
… all this
must already have meant
something to you.
And so, I will not speak.

THE HOMELESS CHILD, SLEEPING ROUGH

"And he passed by on the other side": Luke 10:31

I will not stand unmoved by squirming life and liberty
by mountains losing summits and chain-links
clasping slender arms outstretched.
I will not walk by huddling mass unhindered,
or trample tender fingers trembling, pale,
or step aside on the sweating sidewalk.

Pale fingers poking through the quivering shawl
lifeless, but for flickering eyelids flaying time
and fate and floundering fortune.
Numbed by icy blast of bitter winds
and numberless people passing by,
saving sorrow for tomorrow.

I cannot die the temperate death of feeling
and be afloat like driftwood
on a furious sea.
I dare not wish the nerves stay calm

or that the sails be switched off
in this intimate storm.

But stooping I may find redemption
from my own call to keep walking
past Jesus sleeping wild;
Pause in the midnight of this moment,
feel icy fingers clasping mine,
pulse of my pulse, soul of my very soul.

IN THE RUSH HOUR CROWD,
I SAW HER PASSING BY

In among the faces, I saw her passing by —
coats and hats, collars and eyes,
lips with recent kisses swollen,
lips compressed and slim;
noses flat, straight, turned up or down
and ears white in the cold, even blue.

Buttons holding bodies bursting at the seam,
buttons hardly able to hold the breast within,
buttons below a necktie, beneath a scarf,
buttons blowing careless with the flapping wind,
buttons bold and large and black or bright,
and her buttons, open at the top.

I saw hair and hairdo streaming by,
faces framed gold and white and brown,
even red and green … or purple,
or peeping out in clusters below the hat,
or glistening soft with snowflakes;
and her hair beckoning, black as the starry night.

Eyes, all white at first, then black or brown,
or green or blue looking straight ahead
at nothing particular … or everything.
Eyes, tender, teary, sparkling, laughing,
teasing, languid, bored — a thousand eyes …
and her eyes locked fast with mine, forever.

WHEN I MISS YOU

In the nightfall of dreams, dream on
and tell me the steam still rises
trembling over the darkness.
And then I will wait, eyelids lashing
the wilderness of want and not mind
the hibiscus that blooms hot in the island
of my soulless night. Light blending
with beaten wings, I'll still fly
searing into the noonday sun
and burn with bright flicker
the candle of my melting heart.
Heaven will aid my heaving breast,
seeing I swoon with sweet remembrance
and swell its salty tide with tears.

HE COULD HAVE COME DOWN

He could have come down from the cross
and made a dash for distance between
us and Him and all that he tore Himself
literally to shreds over and goodbye to
blood-sweat and all that
and to sheep and Shepherd
and all that.

There would have been a stir alright,
because one generation would
have remembered
His soft voice and steps
His silver tones and
piercing eyes
and Hands that wrought
life into the clay.

And history would have wept
and known they kept
Eternity trapped in time …
for a while at least

whilst they made hay
and money and happiness
and the Son shone
like never before
into their lives and homes.

And several graves
would have marked
where they lay in splendour
girded with the grand soils
of a million years.
Yearning with them
to be free from
this cycle of so many deaths
and births.

But he stayed
for 3 hours and
a million years.
He stayed and felt
the pulse of the universe
beat in tune with
the pulse of clay
and the death of birth
and death
and the reckoning
of the years.

ADDRESSED TO A TREE CLEARLY ALIVE IN THE DEAD OF WINTER

Speak to me bark, speak before flight
of fight within me and blood congealed;
icy vapours waste the gathering night
and the spirit's cringing casket is sealed.
For then I may breathe and move and see
but will to doting love be dead;
numb, to love's aching misery —
my blood a pale and ghostly red.
Tell me of all the leaves you loose
and the hoarfrost that clothes you;
tell me of the life you choose
still flowing sap strong within you;
and oh! tell me of new plots, new dreams
smothering Spring's still unfrozen streams.

LIVE FREE OR DIE, WAS NEW TO ME

I always thought to die free was liberty,
freedom found within, like fire lighting
the last post, life lived not in longing
for embrace forever of mortal flesh,
but eternity smoking out time,
and today like tomorrow lived abundantly.
Another army with clanging steel
or homing missiles making free,
will soon be bound by tyranny ...
and then our nests of never again
are scattered soon by another eagle
with sharpened talons swooping.
Better far is freedom lived within,
and being freed indeed, be liberty.

STEAM LOCOMOTIVE —
A REMINISCENCE

The steam was forced in screeches
through chimneys clothed in soot;
we sniffed the burning embers and felt
we too could power out from the station
hissing — and straddle the stars at
night or the fiery sun by day.

Black was the colour of life then,
grey the stuff of undying dreams
floating fluffy or fierce across
purple skies — and clouds crumbling
like pastry in wax — heatbright
with grey wick, smoking.

When we high-stepped in and fluttered
like moths before the yellow flames,
it did not touch us and like the three
we laughed in the smouldering light
and chatted with the sweaty engineer
as to an angel.

Sometimes he let us jump and pull
the cable, the whistle-scream rising
with our little screams together and living
like the song of a thousand choirs
in our little souls long after
the song was dead.

Our heads poked out the door,
and red was always green to us,
the signals staring hard and we
staring back, seeing only golden
fields beyond — and a bridge
with gleaming tracks.

We felt imperious looking back —
we were in charge, of course,
of a hundred carriages carrying
crowds of moms and dads
and kids like us, their noses
glum against the window.

We never saw water cold —
only heat and white and hiss
and a silvery stream streaking
vapour over the brooding rails
and willing a mass of metal forward,
with a shout.

The coal was gold and more to us
it glowed yellow alright and stirred
our spirits to crackle of laughter —
sparks sputtering
harmless into the night
and shadows playing upon our faces
like fairies, dancing.

I did not know then of the siren
wailing loud over the mineshaft
and women weeping hysterically;
or of the crowds gathered under
open skies and a gathering gloom,
black as death.

THE BOY BECOMES A MAN

Poplars lined the purple beach
and not a soul in sight.
Golden sky within his reach,
as evening melted into night.
He was twelve and true and tender,
and could be lost (and found) in wonder.

He wondered how the needled pine
could smell so smoky sweet
or how the speckled line
of geese could tuck their feet
so far and wide and high,
and neat into the soaring sky.

He wondered as he sauntered home
his pocket full of sandy shells
how he'd found beneath a dome
of mossy rock and fairy spells
a grotto washed with foamy seas
smooth-kissed by the salty breeze.

He woke and rubbed his eyes
but not in disbelief;
he felt still the golden skies and
in haunting, steep relief the
craggy cliffs, the rising tide.
and the seashells sparkling by his side.

That was a long time ago …
and now the boy's a man —
he feels the same wind blow
and the same, spreading span
of dawn's silken light
slowly kiss away the formless night.

The waves ripple, then roar,
the spray rises from the rocks;
butterflies flutter, then soar
into a familiar sky with flocks
of geese above the flaming trees —
and feet still tucked into the breeze.

Infinite pines still line his way
and tremulous poplars shiver;
green and gold still ring the bay
and fall's carpets gather
softly still, pile on luminous pile,
and purple sands stretch mile on mile.

But the living vision does not last,
he limps back nearly spent —
he feels fall's first wintry blast,
as he slips into his tent.
And sleeps a dreamless sleep
and awakes and begins to weep.

P.T.S.D.

The "enemy" blundered into his bullets
looked but once into his eyes, once only
he saw his little brother's eyes —
soft eyes, moist, misting over, cheeks
ruddy beneath those eyes he *knew*,
now unblinking open wide on the cold grass.

And so the sobbing soldier summons sleep,
speaks softly to it, calls it sweet names …
thinks his feet is off the grieving grass at last;
wills the canopy of shade cover his soul —
then wakes and shouts and weeps aloud,
and screams and swears and cowers.

HE WAS "DEPRESSED" (they said)

"Am I my brother's keeper?"

Drive this drivel from your life, they said,
and in deepest waters, drown it.
Save despair for yourself alone, they said,
and sumptuous sorrow, for no one else.

We have troubles of our own, they said,
why would you stir life's simmering stew?
Why petition worn out souls, they said,
can't you see we're all just getting through?

And so he staggered in the drunken night
staying close, so close to the edge.
Deeper into himself alone he delved,
pestered his dying soul — but no one else.

So when they found him lifeless,
hands splayed out, in a pool of red,
they did not know quite when he had died,
or that weeks ago, he was already dead.

REFLECTIONS ON
THE MARCH OF SORROW

I know your heart was shred and mind benumbed
the better human being dead;
only the smoking sorrows remained
of several seething dreams receding
from the shoreline of shimmering sands.

You believed in lagoons of occasional rest
you believed your boat would not long dock
you believed a restful slumber would seize
respite from noisy remembrances
and failure repeating.

You thought this would not go on
this cannot be endless, and the moon
now on a lonely quest
across a searing sky would give up
and sink at last to rest.

That did not happen and you felt
feeling itself evaporate and fountains
of sparkling white fade and die;
the planned resurrection
rested, and would not be roused.

Such was the seeping darkness
— it seized the soul with stealth;
you tried but could not get away
you fled, but it followed and
shadowed you home.

And did home give you the humble joys
you hoped to find wrapped
in parcels of simple happiness?
a kiss, a word, a hug, a joke
cutting through the icy stillness of the soul?

In actual fact it did!
or you would long be dead.
And over the hugs and tears
that licked your fears
the Cross towered over the wreck.

AMPHIBIAN

Beginnings:

We did not flinch
but cheered when thunder broke
on exploding waters; and laughed
as lightning fell all around us.
When the white light turned grey
and ferocious winds
churned black forms up
ghostly from the ocean's floor;
and hot sands turned wet
beneath our feet.

Such a storm perhaps as stirred the
primordial sea and set scales and fins
drifting land-ward through a million
watery years.
Out-gilled, they crept at last
on ancient sands and slept
in the shade of the sycamore tree.

Awoke … and slept again,
a thousand sleeps,
until at last, it knew, it was.
Its soul now soaring
past the millennial birds
to heaven's very door;
and trembling at spirits unseen
that stalked the slumbering woods.

Tadpole life sperms and
lunges in the dark;
squeezes into spaces —
frenzied swim to span with
a single stroke of luck
a million years in the making.
And then the meeting
in fluid night
and destiny driving division
to organs, limbs and eyes,
to Gandhi, perhaps
or the knave of Deutschland —
oh! the awful life of choice;
or Madam Curie or just
the happy, stunning girl
making his fluid dreams
come true, anew.

Of water mainly she was made,
carried water in her womb —
the babe bent double,
and bathed by the ancient seas;
and then the banks broke
and the waters burst
and perilous groans and pains
marched the babe
through a million years …
until with lusty yells
it greeted the green earth
sans gills, sans feathers, sans tail.

Then as silvery drops slipped daily
through fumbling fingers,
searching in the shallow tub …
it was warned of water's terrors,
yet loved its remembered splash;
and crawling unbidden,
smiling to the river's edge,
until yanked back and scolded
for daring to probe the depths
of icy Pandora —
and the story of its yesterdays.

She later learned to swim,
the length of the deep blue pool;
and plunge into clear waters,
move with slippery fins
and watch as the turncoat toads,
leaped in and out with ease …
and learned to read too,
small books and big,
and Portia's part …
as she mused alone,
on the magic of mercy.

When Fr. Pierre my brother baptized
I was seven and saw it all;
all of us with solemn step
and single file walked clear
of the watery cistern
and settled in our pews;
then there was talk of evil
and Light besting it,
and we said "amen"
a hundred times;
and my mother
beautiful in white
scooped my brother up
my fingers safe
in her other hand;
Fr. Pierre with billowing robe
strode huge in front
until we found the fount.
My brother bawled
when snatched from Mother's arms
and so much water was splashed
that even I felt a few drops
like feathers on my face;
and then he was handed back
and mother bobbed him up and down …
until he smiled.

Why did he yell, I wonder?!
Dry life disturbed and death
of water lived again?
Could be something simpler sure,
like sleep's savage demise
— and loss of chubby cheek on
mother's breast.
Or was it rather loud lament
at being yanked
back to yesterday?

It seemed it was happening —
new birth to another life, his
little body bequeathed
to water, to tears
and emerging triumphant.
But if He who bypassed
the churning millennia,
Himself helpless by Jordan's
Baptist bank appeared …
perhaps my brother,
homo sapiens and all …
needed a dunking too!

When the planets display their
forms of life if any ...
will they regale like Angel's harps
the heavens in perfect harmony,
with stories of watery beginnings?
Evening star or red, (even green),
the quest for water may never find
in these or all the starry skies,
the beginning of all things
in hydrogen inviolate wrapped
with hallowed O_2 held in tight embrace.

But even should forms of life declare
sans water or raindrops or leaves ...
O be strong, my splendid Earth!
For you will outmatch them all
as you begin breathless, bold,
your own story to tell,
of mist and water
your brooding surface covering ...
thundering skies, erupting rain
painting ghostly nations green;
then breaking ice the oceans crashing
and granite grinding slowly
in the salty sea.
And as if this spectacle
were not enough, rewind,
O noble Earth, the brooding years

and show the envious planets
more, so much more …
Stirrings of supple cells
swimming ceaselessly;
then surrender to still more cells,
still more slippery life;
restless journey to another
and *yet* another life, lunging
headlong into the pregnant years;
until at last, erect, aware,
your prize emerged and gazed
upon the gleaming stars in wonder.

Water:

The moon on the waters
is special, he said on bended knee;
better than bluebells blushing
yellow in the twilight; or vertiginous
heights selling sunsets on golden hills.
Much better the deep, dark blue —
cradling the sculpted orb of light
and trembling slightly as he asked
for love eternal in place of love.

Brittle leaves and Northern blasts
release the soaring songs of fall —
whistling rustle, silent frost
and cackling geese returning.
And when winter's snows
subdue the earth in slumber,
and the creeping ice
grows solid on the lake,
we slither, we slide, we skate
over our fossiled past …
frozen at our feet.

The warming suns of Spring
stir sleeping vistas vast
of breaking, shimmering ice and
bare toes testing the softening shore.

Or enormous geese quarrelling
while Cupid's ancient urges surge —
the one screaming for delay
the other following fiercely,
pleading fulfilment …
The one perhaps soaring
with silvery wing away
from certain reminder of
centuries filled with churning seas
and millennia passing before

it found its feathers and could fly …
And the other seeing with urgent call
and fierce summoning
a time of convulsive bliss and soon,
his waddling flock with little feet
shuffling with hastening pace
and in single file approaching
a familiar home?

The call of the sea
brackish on the sailor's lips;
saline in his veins
and casks of ale loaded
in the hold with food
as the ship sets out
from a weeping shore …
women waving bravely,
the salt glistening gold
on their pallid cheeks
and with slender fingers
little children holding fast
to billowing skirts,
lest perhaps they too
are swept like their fathers
into remembered depths
of vanished yesterdays.

It's all very well, very well —
the sailors' frenzy feeding
siren call to sea,
but after the brackish wind
fills first the billowing sail
and fluttering flags are cheered,
long after eager spray of salt
hits supple, straining faces …
saline warm in the sailor's veins,
and cold in the rolling seas,
there must still be water fresh
and held as treasure in the hold —
or the silly songs will cease, the
captain's nose turn sullen,
cry of seagulls seem like thunder,
their serene dives like vultures circling,
fin-like scales from parched lips fall,
love and longing aloud declared,
sins to approaching God confessed,
as delirious terrors of the deep,
awake an ever present past.

They speak of seas so vast
ships by seagulls teased and
furious oceans tossed,
strong nets submerged,
and hauls of a captive past —
the soaking hulls now full,
(but not with men);
flash of lighthouse in the mist
and rocks floundering.
The ships like ghosts
gliding through a thousand ages
and in the human harbour safe.

There are those who yearn
but do not live to see
parched longings meet lips
fiercely moist, urgent red.

But in history's onward sweep
can time itself hold still?
And relive remembrances in the flesh
and march a grand march backward …
Like salmon seething madly
landward, the saline depths forgotten
and for a few weeks remembering
a former time of brooding waters
slowly churning life to land?

Perhaps liking so much what it sees …
crashing waters, streaks of silver
even to the jaws of death …
or slipping past the snapping bears
to clearer streams — slither, splash
a rush of red and onward still;
and in one fell, glorious sweep,
a hero's death in quest
of greater glory — warm bodies
from watery forms emerging,
no matter the cold sea;
love declared perhaps,
and surging sperm
that spawns not a million,
but one or two stripling souls?

We paused upon the burly hill,
felt like Livingstone, all four of us,
— the sea a purple feast below;
all we had pondered plodding
up the sweaty slopes … was here.
Weightless legs launched our charge,
and laughing and leaping we went;
thunderous steps now soft on the sand,
— and four splashes loud in the stillness.
Miles conquered to find this —
naked nipples tickled tight by
feathery waves;
and shimmering salt tingling wet
on lips that taste the ocean's roar.

Homo Sapiens:

In dim, deep, dark waters past,
dense hover, morning mist
and night hushed in …
and it was clearly good;
grander forms appearing
and grind of another age,
groaning for a fairer form …
but still, it was good;
as good perhaps as teeming life
in eager waters loaded,
and moving wide-eyed restless
through the deep …
daring to hope for higher things,
until the leavened land
loosed at last
a lovely, thinking thing …
that lounged with naked skin
beneath the ancient sky …
and it was *very* good.

But what have you O Lord,
upon young earth unleashed!?
Pulled from the churning seas
and upon dry land loosed!
Who roars not like the stalking cat
or trumpeting, lumbering trunk
or even as twittering tribe
of swallows on the trembling tree;
but like the angels sings
songs of a thousand hues
merging to limitless horizons
beyond the sheltering sky.
Or writes of realms seen, unseen,
bleeding a red life into books
that stretches back no doubt
to brackish, heaving seas;
but soars with spirits uncaged
beyond temporal heavens
to perhaps the real thing itself
and receives from there …
an answering call.

The storm that seized the ship
where Crusoe lay asleep —
another mishap merely,
tossed together with stars
exploding and new worlds
spawning newer still.
No design to whistling winds
or waves to spitting fury whipped,
or seeing strong sailors weep aloud
and curse their shattered home?

And yet the creature cast ashore
to a different purpose awoke,
and soon had set about to seek
a shelter from the changing skies,
from rocks, fashion tools
and a fortress home
from skills remembered built.
Like Jane's apes searching
with simple sticks for grub,
he stalked with gun
the island's game —
distant shot, precise,
and steadied tool now smoking.

But did Jane's apes wonder
about a table in the wilderness,
sickness, health, healing,
conscience awoken, repentance,
grace, mercy, justice, peace,
and in the day of trouble, deliverance?
Or of wealth's futility,
money with nothing to buy,
the earth and sea sufficient,
centuries before San Francisco?

Did the apes consider
civilized slaughter bad
as murder — like Crusoe did?
Or that all — savage, slave or free,
from freedom's well drank deep,
… desiring to be free?
Or consider a Friday equal
to himself created,
and courting conscience
better — than many in England?

When soft on the dulcet shore,
we walked together, you and I,
our toes leaving trembling grains
of sand vanishing behind us …
the wind from sea and sky
blew sundrops on our faces
and we wished ourselves adrift —
just you and I on the ocean,
bodies entwined forever …
But only until sundown,
when deepening gold of dusk
would turn us back
to shore — and bring deliverance,
from a familiar night.

She shook a fist at the sun
in the frozen prairie sky,
cried as if in pain …
and cringed for the coast,
where mountains had melted
first out of a smoking sea,
and fringed islands formed.

Now balanced on the bouncing wave
her winning smile was back;
now cradled in a perfect curve
of crashing blue and white,
shoreward she sped,
wrapped and raised aloft
in distant remembrance.

Relentless though the winds
and waves that drove her
back to glittering sands,
again she grasped her board
and with icy fingers fierce
another paddling path
forged through the frothing sea,
and straddled again,
her heaving past.

And yet had lightning rent
a blackened, rumbling sky
and fearsome storm
the churning deep had stirred,
would she not have flown
to familiar, fireside nest —
laughter roaring defiance
and pina colada consumed
with thinking, upright friends?

She recalled some years ago
a flashing fin was seen,
the placid waters piercing,
and people shouted, "shark" …
and soon her mounted steed
felt like quicksand, sinking;
and to a screaming shore
she fled, her paddle lost …
and people reaching out
with blurry arms,
and cheers breaking out …
as she scrambled ashore.

So now with Soul possessed
the spacecraft soars, pierces
the thinning air and peers
at spinning sphere serenely blue,
(and brown and green of course);
but chiefly, soaking blue and brilliant
in the same sun's warming glow
that awoke the dormant seas
to life and still more crawling life …
all those billion years ago.

The waves cannot now prevail —
and boundaries bind our bones
to sand and soil and forest glade
diving butterflies, bees drunk
with scent of springtime buds,
blue skies, silver start and fiery gold.
Darkness to distraction driven
with changing moons and stars
sparkling in the formless deep.
Disease understood and sepsis
silenced, plagues unplugged from
streets with streaming rows of lamps
blazing electric unabashed,
wrought in frothy foam and mist
from the very waters that worked
soberly, silently, and in secret —
churning willing life ever landwards.
Not merely DNA or clay now
of potter of the pondering centuries,
it soars above the craggy tops
of mountains screaming mortality.

Smell of spring rain on smouldering snow
or summer's on the smoking earth,
cracked, broken, begging remembrance
of ordinary beginnings.
Burnt earth, large drops loud
in tingling nostrils breathing deep …
then shimmer of curtains
in tumbling torrents gushing
from the watching heavens
on children slippery, soaked,
leaping, writhing, twisting, turning,
like when they first arrived.

Ferocious deep, but gentle tide
lopping up the soaking sand,
mile on gleaming mile;
distant roar but only crumble
of silvery sounds
rising, rising until its daily roll
of remembrance is done.
And then the grand retreat
reluctant as clasp of lovers —
one more last embrace
and clinging, weak goodbyes ...
then sun and steaming sand,
and barefoot children stepping
on scrunch of a different past;
stooping, stuffng pockets,
skirts, with pearly shells,
exquisite clues to
their own beginnings.
And yet they dare not wade beyond
creeping clear water, tickling toes,
or risk dark oblivion in yesterday —
blue breakers crashing white,
and the churning, shuddering deep.

Frequent the flood waters rose and
she would fight surge
of fierce river raging mad ...
just past high-water mark,
just a little closer to home
and clasp of cold embrace
round slender, straining neck.
The sandbags helped a little
the pumps only a little more
and still she pumped all night
and still the river rose.
The cat in the attic was safe
when the army came to get her ...
she left quietly, crumpled, weary
and weeping upon a soldier's arm —
and still the river swirled and raged
and still the waters rose.

Weeks later she set to work
upon the soggy floor, soaking
the water off, scrubbing until
the tiles with sparkle screeched.
But this was the *seventh* time
the army had been sent to get her
and someone had decreed a stop ...
This time she fought like a tiger,
sobbed and told of struggle to save
for years to build by the river,

the (now) placid, pleading river,
the primitive, ancient river …
There was nothing wrong
with the house itself mind you,
or the gently lapping waves,
or silvery streaks of sunlight
leaping off the scales and fins.

But it was perched on a perilous edge,
close, just too close to oblivion —
and to gills and lungs of yesterday.

With ice-melt it was time to go.
Bodies bronzed and white,
bark canoe splash — and strokes
silver slicing the still night,
tremulous moon and stars afloat.
Hostile seas merely a memory now,
and furs galore upon the far shores.

Barks rose on the river and raced
on the flood with frothy ease
in hollowed, shallow holes colored red
or yellow — or brown as the earth
on which it grew with green
until it yielded to the water, gallantly.

Dawn broke with land looming
dark in the distant West and respite
perhaps from water recurring?
But the bronzed men knew better,
and pointed after a long portage
to swirling rapids they must pass.
Splash, splash again, but this time
the stream reigned supreme, majestic,
unmoved, mindless of their perils,
hustling them along, their paddles
in frenzied foam flaying;
boats turned clean around like leaves
in sudden summer squall.

Hours later they had crossed,
bruised bark in tow, conquering —
as eons ago another creature rose
and clambered to the shore.
Clinging clothes sweltered now
in scorching sun and fire;
and nothing stroked memory
of swirling siren song to oblivion …
save the holes they patched
with spruce gum, slowly.

Portage again! And round a bend
of blistering rocks, they hear the cataract
like distant thunder; like a dangling lure it drew them,
like light celestial bright and brighter,
until at last they stood and stared,
speechless in the chastening spray.
Blast of a thousand cannons continuous,
and atop the rising mist a rainbow
that promised better things —
no backward march to watery beginnings,
no demise of glorious creature — man.

They ate jerky by the dancing rainbow,
and at a point a mile down the river …
shrugged and launched again
and swift down the river, raced away …

From solitary cell perhaps, to a billion more
and on to color, light, tremulous fingers
on quivering strings and symphony;
philosophy fleeing faith — faith, philosophy,
and Apollo met with Selene on the moon.
Even marble figures stately, sublime,
spouting water variously, wrought
in glistening white and many folded wraps,
bashful eyes and breasts beckoning …
sculpted perhaps by single cell turned billions
in seas and storms and land, working urgently
this tale to tell in living stone
with water churning endlessly, yet…
how must the spirit have soared on silvery wings
to turn wood and steel to music
or from slumbering stone to fashion —
Venus rising from the sea!
Or are these mad works perhaps
merely of one cell
turned trillions by the sea?

Loss:

Flesh of his flesh and flight
from very good tree and bad;
salty tears, tender
in soundless sorrow wept.
Say, in deepest, blackest nights
strange skies, stormy terrors …
did it wish for a simpler time?
Of fins and gills and slippery skins,
leaping onto land perhaps
but slipping back,
if scared, even slighted,
and waiting for scramble
of a billion years?
But soul of her soul
and sentient two now one,
all backward thought dismissed …
warm blast and bliss,
throbbing, convulsing life —
and love remembered.

First fruit chiefly water too,
and fall from Eden tasting sweet …
frenzied, writhing heights, then flesh
to drooping flesh, refractory cold …
before firestorm of trials fierce
testing mortal man; crimson drawn
with claw and spear, mingled pink,
even red on Tiber's Roman shores.

But see from fallen forms arising,
out the stirring Aegean sea
swaying maidens on a vase —
sultry in the afternoon,
black and gold, laurel crowns
and rippled gowns now frozen.

Or even from an azure Adriatic
Roman roads from shore to shore,
Sphinxes rising from the Nile,
or out the Ganges temples
chanting "om" to steely skies.

Three nights, three days as nights
swallowed whole and safe,
close to friends unknown
from a million years ago —
and spat out in Nineveh.
We're told he fled obedience
his sole guide instinct,
and sole servant, fate;
with selected outcomes expected,
from years of numberless change.

But what of the guiding Star
that had scripted in his soul,
a different path of nobler deeds —
voyage to another, distant race;
the self sacrificed, plans on hold,
to another purpose prisoner;
like those who wisely followed
another star foolishly,
to an ordinary stable
of new beginnings.

When their lips wet-locked soft,
the sun was about 11 o'clock,
Peonies like sentinels hung
over his grass green pillow,
painting with pink her panting neck;
eager nipple in his palm a prisoner
and soft fingers fumbling all over him …
When it was over, it was still,
pouring sweat out steaming pores
not a green blade stirring;
nearby ants in single file
oblivious of her naked splendour,
scurried silent to and fro.
The first wind was a gentle caress
and the grass still barely moved.
And then like trumpet blast it came
bending the trees in tribute,
rustling with a mighty roar
the quivering leaves and twigs.
And with head to the heavens
she sat up, arms outstretched,
smiling, nipples erect, awoken again.
In frequent, sudden thrusts it came,
symphonic rustle through the trees,
serenading their new embrace,
blue ocean rumble borne
from a hundred miles away
— as when the creature free
from gills and scales at last,

in dry sunshine basked and listened
to the rumbling, rustling ocean's roar.

But at the dawn of its emerging,
did anyone seek to know ...
Will the glorious creature dump,
let slip swift or slow
destiny of its throbbing soul?
And will it eat its likeness man,
fish forms eating fish?
Seek sex ceaselessly
sperm unattended, spewed
into an indifferent sea?
No trembling bodies each to each
no promise of love forever,
no deep gaze for dark eyes
or quiet sobbing at parting?
From foundry earth will it cast cannons,
float ferocious factories on the sea,
make breathing bodies warm blood bleed ...
back cold into the heaving sea?

When Jane's chimps jumped
in rainbow arcs and danced
with thunder and with rain,
and waved their sinewy arms
across the lowing skies ...
Or shook like Samson the trees
that yielded water as they quaked,
Or beat their dripping chests like drums
and made fists and scowling faces
at the splintering clouds ...
Was it their dance of defiance
against a distant history ...
and delirious dance of victory?

And perhaps all this happened too
when Adam's seed first discerned
water in torrents tearing down
the chiselled rocks ...
But this later creature told stories
of remembered joys and dances,
sorrow and the human lot,
suffering understood in part,
and even asked the question, "why?"
It mapped the starry heavens
and the erstwhile seas;
sang singly and together —
of life, of death, of liberty;
contemplated good, evil, mortality,

past, future and all of eternity;
Angelic verses wrote
of love's little day, sad decay,
pestilence and war wasting
generations of the young;
hope's demise and budding promise
postponed for another indifferent day
that seldom came.

There was another Adam needed to
slay the futile cycles,
mingle water and the blood,
rend in twain the curtains,
bring shadowy death to life,
change forever the order of things;
on snowy steed ride in,
with Adam's seed to stable;
turn to purple and still the waters …
and make all things new —
even Jane's splendid chimps.

Like a crumpled rose she cried
when he, unfeeling, left her;
sparkling eyes, lashes long and wet;
eyelids full, collecting grief at first …
then breaking on velvet skin in streams;
and spasms of despair drenching
her quivering lips in sadness.

But even when seawater spray
had stung with salt their laughing lips
they thought nothing of the oceans roar,
or cold clambering up bare skin
of the splashing, haunting tide
as with urgent lips she kissed —
and dreamed of love everlasting.

Who can tell the meaning of
infant's yell on arriving —
there is no knowing what the
baby knows, or feeling what
it feels when tears
flow down its lucent cheeks …

But this we know —
True sorrow tears the soul
of schoolboy screaming injustice,
or the shivering child unable
to quite express its anger
but sobbing quietly in the corner,
tears in big drops making wet,
its brightly coloured dress.
Or with salty tears the troubled teen
raging at love and life itself,
ravenous yearning to escape
beguiling trap and still embrace
of saline past and mortality!

She did not see them lay his
crumpled body in the box,
and when she did see him
he seemed half smiling, asleep
and swamped in blossoms.
The tie was a little loose,
but she could set that right;
his hair brushed back too much?
A gold border wove around the box,
but hardly as bold or bright for her,
as glow of silver white
on clasped fingers,
folded on his breast —
(and held too tight, she thought.)
His cheeks must need some warming,
or why were they so pale?
so she moved a little closer,
her breath like frost upon his brow;
his face when she felt it
was not cool or even cold,
— but sharp as ice.
She shivered a little at first,
only a whimpering, little cry
but when she rose, her eyes
were moist and red and wide.
Her wail when it came at last,
was not a tasteless scream,
but sorrow, despair, anger mixed —

loud and lost, she wept alone …
until the others joined the weeping.

Soon many, many tears were shed,
many cosmic dreams destroyed,
and so many forms of eager life,
dust to crawling dust were ground.

Nobody saw Him squeeze
into this small space of sadness,
nobody knew He felt like nails
her freely tumbling tears,
or heard the tuneless wail
echo mournful off the ceiling.

And they were still weeping together,
when He groaned in the spirit —
and wept.

But when He shouted out
defiant cry at death —
and it came forth bound
with bonds of a million years,
bonds that were loosed at once,
death biting the bitter dust …
Ah, how they marvelled!

Oh, feast of fluids within, without,
life squirming out, squeezed unwilling
to starlight and sunlight, birth compressed
from the restless centuries, reduced
to a few, screaming, writhing hours!

But when dust to dust is pronounced,
the fluids drain first, withdraw
from veins that once surged full,
and from supple skin elastic,
that pulsing pleasures once supplied.

No dew drenching the soft grass
now growing green over the bones
can wake the erstwhile heart
to beat red or even blue,
or start life's strange story again.

All Things New:

You don't want to be here forever
but in a flame, burning, depart
leave bruised egos behind;
water mixed in, streams crimson
and brown and bone still bathed
with rain of remembrance;
until pierced side, water and blood
the cycles cease at last
and we rise together,
to a new tomorrow.

Out on a boat and away
from the pressing throng,
He preached repentance;
and release; and revolution.
And a reminder too,
of humble earlier home
from whence we came?

Walk on water, hand stretched out
and desperate grasp held fast …
"fear not," and no fear now,
of descent back —
to black oblivion.

It was an ordinary well holding stuff
that had stirred soulless
the heaving centuries;
no new sun had seared the skin,
once supple, now parched, asking
for yet another familiar dose of nectar.

Flesh to flesh and five times over
had seemed to her simple exchange
of fluids and now the sixth more exquisite
than the last but still no different
from fierce embrace of fallen Eve.

When the offer came for water
welling up within her forever,
from recurring thirst
setting forever free ...
she spoke of pulley, rope and bucket
and fathomed not how any water
could be drawn, dispensed
without spill, splash, struggle,
and peering deep
into dark beginnings
of dancing, quivering waves.

But then she gazed at Truth
and left her pitcher and ran,
knew the offer was for real,
of shackled past forgiven,
long leap over mortal soup
of a million-odd years —
to long embrace of Love
springing endlessly.

When the Governor asked for water
he would have known of truth
that trembled in the lonesome star
and in luminous faces on the margins
of the famous inn at which
there was no room.
And he would have known of Truth
that had touched the bier —
and turned around,
the amphibious march of death;
and of words that had challenged
the churning centuries …
and not only that, he must have known,
the Truth now standing quiet, serene,
bruised, bleeding, before him …
as he reached for familiar link with
grinding past and mortality —
and washed his hands.

Nothing, night-long caught —
then Figure in dawning mist
and command to starboard cast,
... cast once only and famished nets
now full, the boatmen forbidding
further forays into Tiberias —
turning port, by Life transfixed,
and even splash of naked flesh
plunging into the sea, swimming
away from simpler beginnings
to Life higher than his own ...
majestic on the morning shore
moving the burning coals.
Fire, hunger, then only fossil bones
reminders of forms left behind
— for a greater Form than all.

Of course we must be born of water,
liquid red coursing through our veins,
organs bathed in centuries of saline,
birth through slimy burst of fluid …
and convulsive spasms of desire,
soon discharging screaming life again.

But when will the cycles cease?
When the life-form never thirst?
When forever break its mortal lease?
When depart its mocking hearse?

When Lazarus comes forth it shall be.
When fluids fold in Spirit's fond embrace.
And when death and liquid life recurring —
are stilled eternally.

There must no more be a sea
from which amphibia emerge
or fountains spouting mortality
with dirge on weary, weeping dirge.

No more sun to stir the waters
no more moon reflecting misery,
no more longing for the light,
or midnight recurring night on blasted night.

Instead the creature new,
another birth will know,
a throne, a crystal stream;
sheltering Light, luminous
— and Life in the midst.

Living fountains, living forever,
Bread that abides;
and every tear from every eye
dying on the bloody tree.

PARTING

Fever and furnished fright
and one last leap to longing;
there in the twilight of tomorrow
you stood with stars in your hair;
you made as if to smile but stood
with tears tearing into time;
you made as if to leave
and stayed, staring like sorrow
come to life, our story played out
in your eyes and the swimming
glistening, streaming tide
turning to torrents tumbling,
and teeming torments multiplied ...
Which was when I said enough —
and turned back with you,
into the rising sun.

RECONCILIATION

You were quiet in the car
the button open careless
upon your breast —
and your checked cotton
shirt had carried out,
its caress of consequence,
— shutting me out.

Straight ahead you stared
and not a sideways glance;
you stretched, even squirmed
— but in your own space.
and then you slid your hands
tight beneath your thighs
— and kept them there.

Soon you turned right
and pressed your nose
tight on pleading glass,
your breath frosting the ice,

your neck taut and white,
shoulders curved forward
and glorious breasts, mocking me.

The sobs came quietly —
only a whimper at first
and whisper of rustling leaves
and white stained wet.
But when a flood arose,
I pulled up on the new grass —
and said sorry (though I was right).

YOUR FINGERS WARM IN MINE

The flowers that flourished are finished now,
the flames of summer gone.
The swallow flies high into the distant sky,
and the falling leaf flutters down forlorn.
But *within* the very songs of spring arise
every time I see the fire in your eyes.

The sun whose journey once I charted
as pirate with stolen treasure charts
his flight through sweeping winds fair and foul —
now sinks too soon to rest.
But the twilight on your brow only forebodes
better things, as darkness lengthens night on night.

The grasses green and gushing life,
resurrected from the frozen white,
are withered now, beaten brown and pale
as the skin now blanching pale and cold.
But the promise of the tautness in your breast,
makes my trembling flesh firm up and rise.

Several summers now have come and gone,
several autumn apples crushed sweet and sour.
Several flights of geese have passed
and several evenings shortened into night.
But nothing flies and nothing falls,
while I hold your fingers warm in mine.

TO A HALF-HIDDEN BREAST

If I see all of you, will I wilt and weep
that I had not waited longer?
If I wrap my lips round your peak
will I wish I had stayed longer on the slopes?

If the buttons near your satin skin
had their say would they counsel silence
and point out how
they prefer far
their pining proximity?

Some half of you is open to the world
but a charmed circle seems
to close out my wistful hand
that feign would push
the buttoned border past its post.

ON REFUSING TO COUNTENANCE
MY SMARTPHONE

No, no, I *don't* want to know —
I want to *feel* the hoarfrost grow
to silvery grey upon my sleeve
and freeze my lips with longing.

My lips had hers warm and wet,
when our urgent bodies met.
Our flesh felt taut and hard and soft
and flayed the cringing bed.

I've just hushed her curtains closed
and stepped into starlight stored
for a million years
in twinkling spheres.

And swift on stones like feathers now
my soles fly like a swallow
lost in song — and tears stream hot
against the shivering skies.

And could I for once get lost? —
since I do know the cost
of wandering these half-lit streets
without a glowing map?

And if pricked, bleed a bit
under my white-pressed kit,
and feel pain like burning coal
upon my trembling breast?

And really, *really* I do not wish to know
How the terrors of this night might grow
in the next few, fleeting hours —
(so much colder, on the weather app)

And why must my friends my evening learn
instantly? They should rather earn
the prize of guessing where I was —
or what we did within.

Long now the night of the wandering Soul,
my feet ache and my walk a leisured stroll,
on pavements raw and tender,
but screaming triumph to my toes!

I pass the streetlights one by one,
grey upon black and the night is done;
and oh I see her curtain drawn —
and my flowers upon her window.

REPORTING A PANDEMIC

Dust to dust and doom delivered
by newscasts dripping irony
in considered doses of despair;
feigning knowledge of ignorance,
feigning ignorance of absent panic
and knowledge from experts
claiming uncertainty.

But the web of knowledge weaves
chiffoned layers for me and you and John,
openly uncertain, uncertainly open
to imperfect measure of mortality.
Viral news tempered here
by tantrum of fierce competition
from other news summoned instantly.

I hear the grocer's shelves are bare
I hear that the markets have dived.
A commercial consumes our screens
something about dog biscuits ...
and then I hear as "breaking news"
that we are not to panic ...
that since the last sip of coffee,
another four are dead.

QUARANTINE

When they said you should sink
silent, soulless, to galloping oblivion
fold your wings, flutter of descent
through rooftops from soaring blue,
feathers caught in stifling space,
now quiet, meek, quivering, composed …
they said we were fighting a future
full of foreboding shapes,
dark as night, furtive shadows,
and even a sickle poised to strike.

They did not tell me spring so soon
would soften the snow, the ice,
call the twittering sparrow home,
send chimney smoke in spiralling plumes
toward an ever closer sun;
or that the robin would peck ceaselessly
on the frozen branch at my window —
glorious red on brown and white,
no song yet, but mocking misery
with roving, darting eyes.

ADDRESSED TO A TREE, BURNED
AFTER A RECENT FOREST FIRE

Burned, bruised and broken tree,
shadow of yourself, hope-beaten
ash stricken, twig-shorn, sheltering
with the cowering moss, oblivious
of sun, moon, breeze-shiver,
even of sweet stream sliding
silver and sparkle past you,
repeating ripples nudging
any life left lingering within …
to awake and greet the turning worm.

But you too will soon be swept by cycle
of endless death and dawning life.
Soon your very substance will cease
and in the dust mingle with mould
of a thousand, churning years.

Of course you should not weep
nor wish the many splendored gifts
that graced the springtime of your
youth be turned around like winter again.
From fire new flowers emerge, new earth
turn new twigs, fodder for the next flame.

I must say I take temporal comfort for
troubling, present times from tales
I've been told of life from death and
death from recurring life and think
any life lost will only rise again.

But oh to see your autumn glory
live forever! dancing display of
your particular piece of life
pulsing in its own, particular place forever!
That (and not this) must surely be
the new Heaven, new and fruitful earth …
where the former things are passed away
and behold, all things are new.

TO A LITTLE BIRD THAT
DID NOT LEAVE FOR WINTER

— AND THE BIRD'S REPLY

"Will you not follow flapping feathers
that fight the frigid winds to warmer climes
O little, hopping, flitting bird?
Or flee winter's wake upon fall
and shuffle with restless feet
upon the hardening earth beneath?

Or when leaves from the luminous floor
leap like sparks
with fall's icy blasts
and bigger birds buy time
by huddling close …
don't you think to up and leave?

What about when all around you see
trial flights portending peace
and wide expanse of green —
where here, bare skeletons
of summer beat noisy brown
against the whistling wind?"

"When the skies sleep
a little sooner and the sun
slopes to rest on the golden grass,
I do not fret, I do not dream
of a lingering dusk and summer
dawning endlessly.

I do not fight the frost falling
white upon the flowers
or sleep the restless sleep
of blind ambition —
sorrow at slipping bliss
and fear of tomorrow.

And when first the fluffy flakes
of snow like stars, float in
or soon, as virgin robes
soft cover spring's bashful breast,
I keep on singing —
And wait for consummation."

CANADA WILD ALONE

To be alone, to sink silent to sleep
where the dark grass stood.
And wake with silver streaming deep
into the slumbering wood.

Dreams drip slowly from the stars
but blackest night, yours alone.
Morning meanders in, but nothing mars
the golden light you own.

No one hears the splash of paddle
strike like silk the sparkling lake.
No one hears the canard's crackle
or the answering drake.

The eagle soars the noonday sky,
sees speck of only you.
Or beaver, breaking cover to try
another dive on cue.

Quivering reeds slip slowly past,
unschooled by human hand.
Long and green and yellow and cast
like Cézanne on the sand.

Only you, the moose, the lonely loon
as evening slopes to light —
purple, pink, yellow, gold, maroon …
and day waltzing into night.

THE CLEAN-UP (AFTER A BOMB WAS DROPPED FROM 32,000 FEET)

Sweep the soot softly, the ash
now grey, was a village once …
until blinding light and crash
of beams burning announced
another bomb had arrived.
Seared flesh flew against the walls
and burned together, both derived
from pilot, laughing in the halls,
and stalking the fleeing family.
Limbs and broken bodies
were borne away and silly
sirens have never ceased.
But I see no sign of children sweet
— except in the ashes about your feet.

REMEMBRANCE DAY 2015

Fewer far than the famous names
that speak of severe battles won
with sword and spear and of games
of war played with real shot and gun,
— are the warrior names of Peace
written across the sky in blood
of young men not killed and lease
of life returned where once death stood.
Deep gashes sewn back tenderly
bleeding hearts their beats returned;
even severed heads replaced gingerly
and invite to death and glory spurned.
Their stars are pinned not on starched shirts,
but soar in the skies and spawn a million births.

THE SERIOUS SPOUSAL FIGHT
(WHEN ALL SEEMS LOST)

Beyond the boisterous noises counselling death
beyond the beaten hopes piled hideous at your feet.
Beyond the brine-soaked eyelids saving burst
of next torrent for new tissues, newly snatched;
just beyond, and glittering in the yesterdays
of your yearnings, the slippery shores of safety
bob up and down, cork on a cascading sea.

You cannot see the pummelled past, the present
painting battered canvas, every last corner,
with cringing colour red — blocking over blue and
the green grass, yellow daffodils, even grey skies
that brightened brilliantly with arc of light and rain.
And of course, tomorrow does not even tempt
the tenderized flesh — spiced, salted, seasoned,
and ready now for present, roaring fire.

How dark this deepest night seems to be,
how nimble every demon, dodging sense,
churning the cauldron of doubt, darting about
and pulling memory's golden shutters down!
How flies the store of sorrow together tamed,
or heartfelt joy, felt beat on alternate beat;
how dissolves laughter's leaven, or remembrance
of locked embrace and recurring ecstasies!

And still, just beyond the flailing soul,
a few strong strokes away, but ever in sight,
the shimmering shoreline slips slowly by,
until it too is swallowed by quiet despair.
Quiet and sinking now, the fight surrendered,
Limp arms lowered to your sides and then …
a surge of strength as Grace steps in
and trembling fingers grasp the solid Rock.

THE PAUSE
(THAT BIRDS MAKE BEFORE FLIGHT)

Spring-time and song-time, tilted head held steady,
soaring flight or short foray,
silver gleams of moving heat from moving leaves
or dawn leaching light from leavening skies ...

And still the flashing eyes stealing time
one, sharp, brief, stolen moment —
then flutter of diminishing wings
marking the heavy air with height and heat.

Perhaps considering with fevered breath
the dull colors of death —
human death or human misery,
or fluttering, moving, feathery, flying sorrow?

Or making hay of memory of lavender fields
left blooming in the South —
ere memory itself be soon snuffed out
in flights across the wintery fields?

Yet when taught and tamed and fed,
the darting eyes are gone,
gone sharp shiver of body,
tapping feet and pounding heart.

Quivering claws perched with perfect poise
replaced with restful, hopping ease.
and oblivious, fawning eyes, in place —
of wild gazes shot through the still air.

RESILIENCE

Ice crunch crashed call to spring
when winter's melt froze over;
swallows ceased their flight
and chattered of chimeras
chiselled from icy cliffs —
and crystal flow now stilled.

Was it hope flying high
that hopped frozen again
on the grinding ice?
Or made mournful sounds
for song or sought in silence
signs from the frozen winds?

Visions more vivid than dreams
dashed on the blowing snow
must have held them fast …
Or why did they chatter again
on cool but warming breeze
of coming consummation?

DETACHMENT

Reeds on the river rustling,
what rest you have known!
Careless on the banks arriving,
unheralded, unsung, unknown!
But how the rusty bells of morning rang
when we arrived, and how the choirs sang!

Straight up and seeking the sun,
race your blades of gladness green.
No battles fought, victories won,
no sinews straining to be seen!
But how we fight and how the angels weep,
to hear us speaking vengeance in our sleep!

Night steals in with noiseless stealth
and never do you shout or stir.
Darkness descends black as death,
yet never drives you to despair.
But oh, what fearful cries we mortals make
when death arrives and parting's pangs awake.

Storms beat ceaseless year on year
on your graceful, swaying sides.
Yet no chorus of complaint will appear
or rise with the rising tides.
But oh, how high our heaving bosoms rise
when the dreams depart and the music dies.

Fellow reeds don't make you falter
or shake the fist with rage.
You remain a very rock of Gibraltar,
no axe to grind or war to wage …
But can you love as we humans do?
Or kiss with lips locked fast, forever true?

MUSTANG

I took my muscled horse today
through fields both gold and brown
It snorted, sniffed and grunted
— and stormed out of town.

I sat in the saddle and saw
the snow on the mountains afar
and over above and hanging bright,
the bashful, evening star.

It could keep me warm and toasty
though the frost was ever near
why, it could even cool me down
in this, it had no peer!

I passed cows and rolling meadows
and shuffling sheep on the green;
soon a deer darted into sight
and sped away seen, unseen.

It raced the speckled birds,
it startled some to flight,
yet if they ever crossed its path,
— they got away alright!

When dark clouds gathered thick,
and down came hail and rain
— it kept me dry, it kept me safe,
I felt I was in sunny Spain!

The rainbow stretched a colored bow
right across the lifting grey;
my horse rode right through the mist
and the sunlit, sparkling spray.

Soon it sensed I was a little tired,
and sang a soulful song for me!
and when evening shadows fell
it was even playing Tchaikovsky!

I rode it right beside my humble home
and stepped out on the ground
and while I stroked and patted it,
— it uttered not a sound!

THE CONDITIONAL ARTIST

Only the torrent must tumble again,
sparkle on silvery stream …
for the grass is green already,
bright bugs crawl the fertile earth
and little white flowers weep dewdrops
every morning as I wander by,
and walk the dry riverbed
bleeding the pregnant hours
of life and love and liberty,
and visions written on a bold new sky.

All else is lined up and in sync,
summer's songs are heard
from every swaying branch;
and the bluebird breathes fire
as it singes the deep blue sky.
Even the skin is blushed just right
from hours in gently blowing breezes
spent searching the restless Soul …
If only I'd feel cool waters about my feet,
and the blasted river would run again!

To think nothing of dying brother
cradled in tired arms, dying;
and hours spent honing the hour
of knowing he must die too.
A world at odds with his immortal bird
not born for earth's hungry generations.
Burning desire — and Beauty
captive in a neighbour's walls …
And his spirit soaring to heaven's door,
in this, his miraculous year!

The clock was set too late today,
so I banged it down with spite;
the week was weary with well doing,
yet moist lips had kissed me to sleep.
The darkening skies spoke thunder,
but now a flood of fearful phantoms
moved fast into the river's muddy flow.
A headache had seized my muddled head
when I reached furiously for my pen
and holding my head, I wrote.

SEEING SONGS AND HEARING BLUE

I heard blue, saw noises, felt the morning ripe
to snatch from it a song,
and knew this must be how the poets redeemed
eternity from time.
They would have heard heartache in the clouds,
brought it down to ground;
they would have seen spring's cool breezes brisk
and cool upon their brows.

They would have lingered long enough to taste
red on their noses
even with cheeky flight of single robin streaking
across a fragrant sky.
They would have heard grass growing green
over wintry brown
and seen voiceless sighs
in a poem.

SONNET TO MYSELF

When I stood in the studio and wept,
it was not because I could not hear hope
whistling in the whirlwind, or cope
with the way I washed or dressed or slept.
I had spent a splendid fortnight writing verse,
I had dreamt dreams of destiny and light;
I had tickled Beauty into fabled flight
of fantasy — lines tight and true and terse.
With wide open windows I had looked out
and seen people streaming slowly by,
and like Shalott's lady I had started to cry,
seized with sadness, fright and doubt …
until, that is, the children charged in,
and examining my lines … began to grin.

DREAMS

Dreams deceive, dreams deceive, they die
with the morning light; and the dreaded
song that serenades your sleep —
symphony of love, drumbeat of death,
ambition's soaring notes
and clash of a thousand cymbals speaking hope —
simmer in the cauldron of tomorrow ... and cease.

Dreams you love to forget on waking,
terror, soundless cries and trembling knees;
forms fantastic, dragons breathing fire,
fearless prophets foretelling private doom
... these are like the vapour too,
on a crisp morning, dissolving.

The present is its own dream,
gifted with gold and myrrh and
glory; twenty-four hours of triumph,
leading dreams of yesterday and
tomorrow chained, captive in its train,
proclaiming fulfilled possibilities, silently.

THE DAY AFTER (the loss of love)

Mostly languor and listless sorrow
from every crevice seeping silently.
But oh, how many breaches in the dykes!
Eyes now misting, now moist —
creeping tide turning soon to salty torrent.

Mostly the light turning liquid on the face
and wakeful walk upon the grass grinding
to uncertain halt, foot stubbing the earth
with pointless certainty and hovering gnat
with fearsome ferocity struck down.

Mostly the looking into long lost sea
and gazing upon the cresting boats
until sea and sky merge in glittering line
while sunken toe in sandy well
tells drowning tale of deepening grief.

Mostly the sinking into moist grass
green but gaping like the grave;
yet soft upon the body seated warm,
some strength returning surprising,
then sinking again in several, wintry sighs.

Sometimes the rising from the ground
before the blackening sky seeks darkness;
sometimes the elbow levered up,
uncertain steps past sheltering sorrow —
a shake, a little shiver, then a shout.

TO THE MODERN SINGER
- A CYNICAL SONNET

Futile the feverish sweep for certainty
and the fool will forage there for fame,
endlessly see visions, a promised city
floating in forever with his name
emblazoned across the sky in gold.
Fawning crowds falling prostrate
in the way and all the tickets sold,
to all his shows and soon a state
is reached when he can do no wrong,
not a star of all the stars that shine
can outshine or come near his song
or pour with passion, so sweet a wine.
Poor beggar still, outside the city gates
pleading success as success waits.

NIGHT ON A SUMMER'S DAY

Longer and longer and later,
lingering light and shimmering sky.
But morning's twitter turns to twilight
soon, so soon, as the music stops.

Quite early still and many hours remain,
and many more, now it's summer.
While golden sunbeams turn to silver,
and early clouds creep upon the silver sun.

Not quite noon yet, yet almost night within;
not quite lunchtime, yet dinner denied.
Beguiling flavours float in on the sultry breeze,
past hunger, thirst and flickering light.

Last few flickers of feeling, then numbness
and curtain call, smoke of smouldering embers
snuffing duty out; destiny now enslaved
and meekly following mediocrity in tow.

Twilight true arriving, the tears now flow,
watering gardens of unwavering doubt.
Salty streams arise, the oceans roar
and finally, the struggling Spirit sinks.

"Master, I drown, dark despair drives night
into morning and shadows to noonday sun.
I perish … and no one shall even notice,
the bubbles on the heaving brim."

"But ah! I saw you floundering on the waves
I saw your morning's rapid slide to night
I felt your numbness — and when you stared
blankly at the stars … I was there!"

Those thrashing arms now cease their flaying,
dreams revive and walk on water.
This fearful night to sheltering noonday turns
and a great calm on your destiny alights.

THE PRICE OF LOVE

The tears I shed don't matter, now
nor the heart that faster, fuller beats.
Or the rising sobs that steal my breath,
or my quivering, cowering lips …
See how your eyes speak despair too,
and your breasts taste salty, wet,
dewdrops dance upon your neck
and dribble like a dirge.

We knew our feet would follow
this trail of trials together;
we knew our hearts were bound
with links of gold forever.
How moans the whispering grove now
that serenaded once our dancing steps!
How sleep the stars in darkness now
that sparkled like garlands above us!

It started with me, I know, this mess —
my tale of misery that made your cry,
played havoc with our bonded Souls,
and brought us to this sorry pass.
But once the price of love is paid,
and the gnashing noises cease,
the grey will morph to golden dawn —
and we'll rise together from our knees.

HORIZON

Blue on brown the line recedes,
as bow of many colours dives
into the border, speeds
our many splendoured lives
into the prescient present —
straining at ropes that seek
to bind us to a past that went
whistling by, ere we could speak
and tell how we wept floods
of futile tears at its passing;
and hope now for better buds
our futures caressing?
— Better to wait patiently for night
and keep our restless feet firmly in sight.

NOTE TO MYSELF,
AT SEVEN IN THE MORNING

Sleep a little longer, don't dress the dawn
with counterfeit garments that glitter gold
but hide deep shadows fold on fawning fold;
wait a little longer to taste the morning tea,
bitter on your lips, cookie crumble sweet,
eyes forlorn, blank upon the busy street.

Don't touch that toothbrush yet, lips trembling
fingers fumbling, stroke on absent stroke
and pangs of regret, poke on bristly poke.
Keep the shower waiting, or torrent of water
may hit you hot upon your bruised back,
pile on sorrow, whack on watery whack.

And why would you feel about for clothes
and walk willing into the certain storm
when naked now under the sheets and warm?
Or eat porridge pilfered from towering shelf,
milk coaxed quivering from the can,
crackling eggs croaking on the pan?

Remember the tears still damp upon the pillow,
how they came like rain and would not cease,
soaking linen, crease on cringing crease.
Remember how you fell asleep at three
and slept till seven an infant's sleep …
and you would wake up now and weep?

OUR BROKEN DREAMS

Like shipwrecked shards upon the shivering foam
our broken dreams heave lifelessly;
soaking in wet despair, dripping salty tears,
and drenched with despair.

Oh how we loved the lingering sky
on fields of lavender laced with gold!
And do you remember now
how we stood there and wept?

Wept perhaps for winter waiting
upon its windswept wings?
Or even for fall filtering in so soon after
summer's sun had scarcely soaked us?

We gazed upon fall's golden skies
and watched the flocks fly darkly past;
we sought the dew-drenched darkness,
we thought the stars were in our grasp.

Much later we learned the silver morn
did not always creep upon the gold;
or always light the yellow fires of fall
or gleam like lanterns through the leaves.

Instead, a windswept hillside awaited us,
with Sisyphus straining at the rock;
we joined him in the grey and beating rain —
and talked of the summit ceaselessly.

And then we looked and saw the stone,
slip away with thunderous sounds.
And we paused, but kept on walking —
toward another dawn.

BRANTA CANADENSIS

"No, no do not go — though
green grasses yellow grow
and field flowers fade;
there is frost now in the shade
and the breezes blow ice.

Think, in going you must make
a thousand miles by day, awake;
sleep in alien fields of stubble
and fly straight again into rumble
of thunder and wintry storm.

And do you really wish to make a "V"
over lands seething with misery?
or trumpet and honk and cackle
when there is whisper and rankle
of gossip and intrigue below?"

"Oh I must go and you will stay
for whether by the sun by day
or the blinding snow by night
I'll soar into the morning light
and even over brooding mountain tops.

We do not treasure the things
you do; and on dappled wings
carry only the crisp air
made golden in the glare
of sunbeams that bend toward us.

We glide far above human blood
that flows more furious than flood
of rivers we pass peacefully over;
we dare not fly any lower —
or blood may from flesh draw blood.

We dream of love that lasts forever
we live the dream too, and weather
pain and pleasure, flock and brood,
with the same lover who stood
in the tall grass as we first made love."

It was speaking still, when the shot rang out
a pause, a shriek; and then a shout
of hideous human sounds; a flutter
full of grace, beating wings, and stutter
of cackles fading to silent wrath.

O unfeeling, foolish, stupid man!
O life that takes life because it can!
O bloody shot that just made a widow
now flying stunned into the twilight's glow
and weeping a better life than ours.

ANOTHER RECKONING
(for awards, orders, prizes)

Another reckoning, another applause,
another jury, another judge,
and another warrior fighting peace
in shallow, frothing, swooning lives
awarding prizes like pumpkins —
glowing, but hollow
in a very dark night.

There must be a real order
rewarding crosses borne joyfully,
trials to triumph daily turned;
shouldered burdens turning light,
yoke exchanged and rest.

And change delivered *now* —
bleeding, bruised, raw,
blinkers off, smart about-turn,
fleeting glitter abolished,
humility seized and reward
of several candles burning
in several dark corners
seared in ethereal flame.

GROWTH

With feline grace he swooped
upon the stillborn task,
stirred stupor to life,
streaked across the stars,
and stalked his lively prey, success.

He told me he was strong,
he told me he was burning
with a brighter light.
He told me he was teasing
the very night.

But it was a very black night
and he felt a hundred noises,
upon him, closing;
and he fled, clear in sight
of his scampering prey.

Rumble of thunder as he ran,
light and water, then a flood,
and the night like a cage
closed like death around him
and then … the tiredness came.

A little at first and fitted
with easeful rest,
its own flirtatious escape;
the quarry still before him,
but further as it fled.

When he lost sight of it
deep into the callous night,
it was very cold indeed
as he stood in his shoes,
and he shivered.

Where were the dreams of yesterday?
Where was the kiss of fame?
Where the taming
of the night
and the seizing of the prey?

He breathed sadness now
and feared the folly of his chase
and it was with fear he laid
his head upon the grass
of yet another day.

The dew then woke him
from his dreamless sleep.
He found his strength return
he raised a hand up to the heavens
and his body to the morning breeze.

In the distance gleaming white
his quarry seeming lifeless lay,
he looked at it with longing,
and as he stepped slowly up to it
it stirred and moved away.

"SUFFICIENT UNTO THE DAY"

"Take therefore no thought for the morrow: for the morrow shall take thought for the things of itself. Sufficient unto the day is the evil thereof."

Yeah, tear into the heart of tomorrow
and taste the stormy tumult there.
Drink deep the draughts of sorrow
and splendid despair!
For to think only of today
is not in our dumb DNA!

We must know what company
the moon in mystery keeps.
The stars must sparkle and foresee
while the orb in darkness sleeps.
Although we know of stars that fall
and do not influence us at all!

How slight the shade before our eyes
that shields us from tomorrow's glare!
How hard the sighing bosom tries
to strip tomorrow's cupboards bare —
peering through foreboding pain
and feeling now, the forecast of rain!

The eagle soaring today's sky,
swoops, gathers and soars again.
No fearsome talon, piercing eye
will tomorrow's hunt proclaim.
But we with fretting, fevered brow
must soar beyond the here and now!

Dreams of yesterday bad enough,
blend with tomorrow's useless yearnings.
For you see, we're tall and strong and tough
and will not wilt or lose our bearings! ...
Until sorrow rushing like a flood,
drowns out hope and nips it in the bud.

SEA WALL

Vancouver, 2014

Ceaseless silver now,
steep upon the shimmering rock
And would you have guessed
hell in heaven sublime perched
on floor no. 36, looking down,
way down — staggering sorrow
piled pill on pleading pill, fidelity
through fancy windows flown,
casement cringing the dark night,
night on night?

And then, this magnificent aura
of churning ease, indifference
sharpening its claws on the
weeping cliffs and crying, "shame
she left you, shame!"
The walk (what "walk" is this?),
upon the unfeeling shore,
cool waters, turning cold and
bringing winter in, wave on wave.

The spray white and caking
on his freezing cheek,
and face entombed with fright.
If waters deep as deepest blue
and rocks with rousing chorus
of crescendo sound …
are all oblivious to his pain;
even the little boats with sails,
bobbing like birthday balloons,
even the blue hills that rise
sheer and blue on green,
even the pebbles round,
and smooth as her breast …
if all these fail to douse
the fire in his breast,
he may well feel his fate
to be bound
with the boundless sea —
unless, that is, an arm round about him
stops him, and makes
· the proposed plunge irrelevant.

AT EVERY TURN

At every turn I saw him
from the velvet of the rose,
to the teeming wilderness.
From bounding brook he whispered
and from deepest deep
a soulful silence sliced
through the lurid tempests
that raged within my soul.

And I saw him in the leaves
of the books of the philosophers
and the dusty drumbeat of death
explained in myriad ways.
I saw him in the skies
waving with the wind, furiously;
and in the doleful thunder
deafening out the sounds of reason.

I saw him fretfully pacing
the sunlit patios of our rest
and stirring my soul with
secret longings for yesterday.
And today I saw him sitting
next to me and say:
"what a ride it's been —
you and I
on this tired horse together!"

HUSH, HUSH THE SNOW FALLS

(A hundred years ago)

The snow fell quietly in the early night
and all was hushed without, within;
snowflakes and shadows in serene flight
alighting in feathery layers of white
and floating free on the crisp, virgin
air; And then, it was still, how still!
Not a leaf moved or stirred upon the hill.

And then you wouldn't think the snow
was all white for it glowed and gleamed
yellow and gold and silver; you could blow
up a fistful of white and you would know
the gold-dust flew light and beamed
back shining colours; roofs came alive
and rafters sparkled in the drive.

Morning dawned delightful as a dream
the mountains white and brown and green;
the lake was lapping the layered cream
from the frozen shore as a team
of horses rode into the sheen.
Snow falling like manna in morning flight
and every window framed in feathery white.

EMMAUS

Every homeward step like summer's spring
— sedate, infused with newness, settled,
but scrambling for new and urgent life.
The dust cool upon the skin,
and one sparrow another chasing
into a newly bemused sky ...
Dusk's shadows scarcely heeding the miles,
the miles, scarcely the darkness heeding.

Had he not heard of flayed flesh,
Roman nails, Jewish tomb now empty?
Had they not heard of love multiplied
or death's demise foretold?
And as mortal mules, camels, travellers
passed them by, he too would have gone,
melted into death of spring ...
but he was asked to stay.

The cold stone walls now held
another dispensation unaware;
bread in clay oven baked;
hands lately pierced,
by love immobilized, now free
to break the clay-wrought bread.
Three of them, then only two —
another Kingdom dawning;
and two burning hearts
upon the way remembered.

Francis Christian is a poet and a surgeon — the
former ever since his adolescence and throughout
his adult life; the latter, an aspiration and a goal ever
since he entered medical school. After completing his
medical and surgical training in India and in England,
he did further surgical training in Canada and is now
Clinical Professor of Surgery in Saskatoon, a city in
Western Canada.

He is the co-founder and director of the Surgical Humanities Program in the University of Saskatchewan. The program seeks to engage medical students, residents, and surgeons with the humanities in a way that enriches and informs their practice of medicine. He is also the editor of the *Journal of The Surgical Humanities.*

Francis Christian says of his poetry: "Such consequential and searing experiences as love and beauty in our universe, must have the thread of eternity running through them. A certain deep sensibility, like notes however faintly heard from an Angel's harp, assures us that this is so. I hope my poems will awaken for the reader this precious sensibility, never far from us and always reminding us of that which we cannot yet clearly see." Dr. Christian has been writing poems since his adolescence, and he sees poetry and surgery as the right and left arms of his being.

His writing offers breadth and diversity to the intimate connection between art and health that is core to HARP's mission. Through his poetry he enters profoundly into the bodies and minds and souls of suffering humanity, juxtaposing unconditional love with moments of telling irony. His longer poems recount stories of sensuality and beauty, evoking frequent biblical and classical images, and exploring humanity's very origins, wanderings, and often hidden purpose.